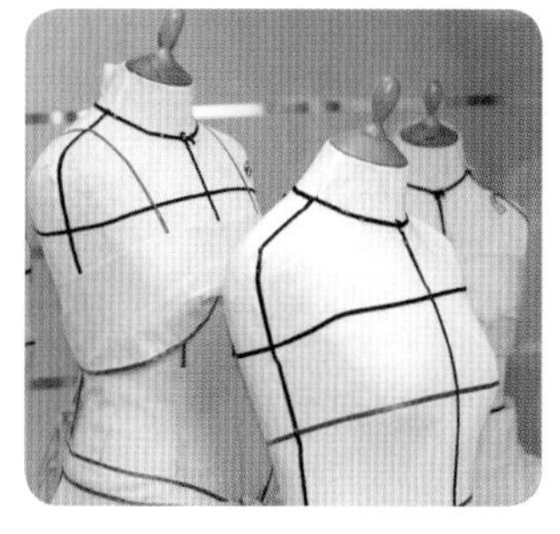

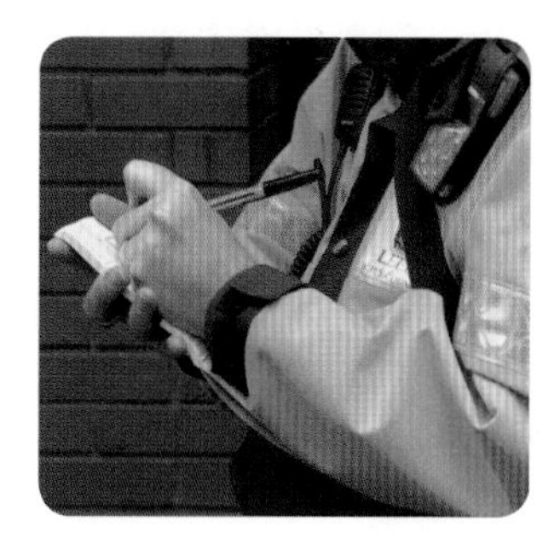

STUDENT GUIDE

Level 1 and 2 Projects

Level 1 Foundation Project | Level 2 Higher Project

Coordinating editors: Elizabeth Swinbank and John Taylor

A PEARSON COMPANY

Pearson Education
Edinburgh Gate
Harlow
Essex
CM20 2JE

First published in 2009

ISBN: 978-1-84690-364-9

Printed and bound in China (GCC/02)
Picture Research by: Thelma Gilbert and Sally Cole
Index by Jane Read
Typeset by Steve Moulds, DSM Partenership

This Project Guide is accompanied by a Teacher Resource Disc. All the authors listed below have contributed to one or both publications.

Authors

John Taylor (a chief examiner)	Rugby School
Charlie Barclay (a principal moderator)	Marlborough College, Wilts
Tony Darby	Rugby School
Diane Goff (a chair of examiners)	Hillview School for Girls, Tonbridge, Kent
Ian Marcouse Director	A-Z Business Training and Lambeth College, London
Graham Meredith (a principal moderator)	
Elizabeth Swinbank	Department of Educational Studies, University of York
Helen Turner (a principal moderator)	Act On It

Acknowledgements

Parts of this Project Guide and Teacher Resource Disc are based on the Level 3 Extended Project Student Guide and Teacher Resource Disc (Edexcel, 2009) and incorporate the work of the following authors:

John Taylor
Elizabeth Swinbank
Andrew Smith
Michael Reiss
Peter Richard
Graham Meredith
David Harrison
Peter Ellis

We also wish to thank the following for advice, assistance and support

Barbara Almond	Rugby School
Sandra Wilmott	University of York

Images: The publisher would like to thank the following for their kind permission to reproduce their photographs:

(Key: b-bottom; c-centre; l-left; r-right; t-top)

Alamy Images: World Religions Photo Library 30; Jacky Chapman 37b; Sally Greenhill 12; Angela Hampton 14; Martin Ruegner 28; Steve Skjold 55; H. Mark Weidman 24; Bridgeman Art Library Ltd: Private Collection/ Giraudon 52; Corbis: 60; **DK Images**: 22, 37t, 40; Pearson Education Ltd: 42; Punchstock 59; Rex Features: 8; **Science Photo Library Ltd:** Robert Brook 33; Christian Darkin 29; Maximilian Stock 48; **Amy Page**: 56;

Cover images: **iStockphoto**: Christine Balderas cl (hammer), tr (doctor); bluestocking tc (calculator); **Ronald Hudson** cr (parking ticket); Sergey Kashkin br (food serving); Kuzma tc (hard hat); Luca Manieri cr (plants); Martin McElligott bc (baking); Vladislav Mitic cl (tailors dummies); Dusan Zidar tl (haircut); Krzysztof Zmij bl (microchip); **Masterfile UK Ltd**: David Muir b (painters easel)

CONTENTS

Introduction to the Level 1 and 2 Project Guide

About projects

If you are using this book, you will almost certainly be working for a Project qualification, either as part of a Level 1 or 2 Diploma or as a stand-alone qualification equivalent to half a GCSE.

A Project a major piece of individual work in which you explore a topic or a question that is of particular interest to you. You will either be making something (an artefact), be involved in putting on an event, or exploring a topic through a research question.

A Project is not simply a piece of coursework. Rather, it should extend your knowledge and skills in ways that are challenging and new to you. During your Project you will be learning new knowledge, developing new skills, and bringing together skills and ideas from different subject areas.

For your Project you will need to:

- choose a topic
- specify an objective (say what you intend to achieve)
- plan how you will reach your objective
- carry out some research
- use suitable techniques to reach your objective
- carry your project through to the end
- share the outcome with other people
- review and evaluate your progress.

This book guides you through all these stages of your Project.

About this book

Before starting the main work for your Project, you will need to develop some general skills that you will use and demonstrate during your Project work. Chapters 1 and 2 of this Guide are about developing these skills of research and thinking. The book itself provides only the bare bones and you will probably be doing more activities relating to your Diploma, or your GCSE subjects, and to the eventual topic of your Project. The Teacher Resource Disc (TRD) that accompanies this Guide supports many such activities.

Chapter 3 of the Guide is about choosing your project topic. When you have developed a range of skills, and explored some interesting areas, you can decide what you are going to do for your Project and complete your Project Proposal Form. You will then need to plan your Project and begin to build up a record of your work. Chapter 3 helps you do this.

Chapter 4 takes you through your main Project work and shows how you can develop your skills and build up a written report one section at a time.

Finally Chapter 5 takes you through the final stage of your Project, where you need to communicate your work and review your progress.

Each chapter of this Project Guide includes the following features.

Main text

The book sets out some information and discusses ideas relating to project work. Each chapter is divided into lessons – which may, or may not, coincide with the actual sessions arranged by your teacher/tutor/lecturer.

In the main text, some words are printed in bold. These are key terms relating to project work, and are defined in the Glossary printed at the back of this book.

Activities

a5: EVALUATING AN INFORMATION SOURCE IE CT

Choose a magazine article, a leaflet or a website with information on a topic that you are interested in and carry out an evaluation using the questions listed above.

The book includes many *Activities*. Some of these are for individual work, while others are for groups. You will probably be asked to do some of these activities in class or for homework.

Icons

In the Activity and Project Springboard boxes, there are blue and green buttons with letters on them. The blue buttons show which of the three Functional Skills the activity helps you achieve:

English 

ICT 

Mathematics

The green buttons show which of the Personal, Learning and Thinking Skills (PLTS) the activity helps you acquire. PLTS are an essential part of the Diploma. Here is what they represent:

- IE Independent enquirers
- TW Team workers
- CT Creative thinkers
- SM Self-managers
- RL Reflexive learners
- EP Effective participators

Project hints

These alert you to points that will help you gain good marks for your project.

PROJECT HINT

Using your own questionnaire to collect information for your Project will help you to demonstrate good research skills.

Project springboards

In various places you will find Project springboards. These include suggestions for areas that might be developed into projects.

PROJECT SPRINGBOARD

Studying artefacts made by other people might give you some ideas for your own Project.

Course references

Course references direct you to relevant activities, lessons, or chapters elsewhere in this book.

COURSE REF.

See Lesson 1.1 for some suggestions about information sources.

1 Gathering information

1.1 What do you want to know?

Figure 1.1
Asking questions

PROJECT HINT

Use the '5 W' questions when looking for information for your Project.

Asking questions

One of the first things you will need to do for your Project is to find out some information. In other words, you must do some **research**. To do this, you have to ask questions (Figure 1.1). Asking the right questions can help you find the information you need. It's a good idea to decide on your questions before you start, so that you don't forget and leave something out.

When finding out about an event, it is useful to start with the '5 W' questions:

- *What* happened?
- *Who* were the people involved?
- *When* did it happen?
- *Where* did it happen?
- *Why* did it happen?

The answers to the '5 W' questions might help you decide what else to ask.

a1: FINDING ANSWERS

Read a report of a recent event and practise answering the '5 W' questions. It could be a sporting occasion or a celebrity event and need not be related to your Project area.

Sources of information

Some of the research you do for your Project will be **primary research**. This is research that you do yourself. For example, you might use a questionnaire that you have thought up yourself, or you might make some measurements, or collect the results from your own experiments.

Your Project will also include some **secondary research**. This means finding out about work that other people have done.

For your Project, you will need to gather information in a variety of ways from a range of **sources.** Here are some examples of ways that you might research information for your Project:

- Reading
  - books
  - magazines
  - newspaper articles
  - websites
- Observations at places of interest
  - museum
  - workplace
  - theatre
  - laboratory
- Collecting sample materials
- Making measurements
- Questionnaires and interviews
  - members of your class or your centre
  - your teacher/tutor
  - experts in your project topic
- Watching and listening
  - TV programmes
  - films
  - CDs

PROJECT HINT

Using a range of sources for your Project (not just websites) will help you demonstrate good research skills.

a2: PRIMARY OR SECONDARY?

IE

For each type of source in the list, say whether you think it would be most useful for primary research, secondary research, or both.

Keep a record

PROJECT HINT

When researching for your Project, keep your Research Record Sheets and include them at the back of your Project report.

When you carry out your research, make sure you keep a record. For secondary research you could use a Research Record Sheet like the one in Figure 1.2. Put your name on the sheet and the date you did the research. In case you or anyone else want to go back and check the information, record details of the source. Use these headings – notice that three of the 'W' questions are used here.

- Title of source

For websites, include the url.

- *What* is it?

Book, website, newspaper, TV programme, etc.

- *Who* produced it?

Names of people and/or organisations.

For books and magazines list the publishers as well as writers.

- *When* was it produced?

For books and magazines, this is the date of publication. Look at the title page near the front of a book.

Some websites give the date when they were last updated. If they do not, record the date when you visited the site.

a3: KEEP A RECORD

Using *two* different sources from the list, find out some information about a topic that you find interesting. For each of your sources, use a Research Record Sheet for your answers to the '5 W' questions and for details of your source.

1.2 How good are your sources?

Correct and complete?

When you do your Project, you will be gathering information from several sources (Figure 1.3). Some sources are better and more reliable than others. A good researcher is someone who can **evaluate** their sources – that is, say whether they can trust them to provide correct and complete information, and why.

Research Record Sheet

Name *Mil Smith* **Date** *24 February 2009*

Source

Title — *Airplane crash lands into Hudson River*

url — *http://edition.cnn.com/2009/US/01/15/new.york.plane.crash/*

What is it? — *Website*

Who produced it? — *CNN US news broadcast company*

When was it produced? — *15 January 2009*

Information

What happened?

US Airways plane landed in river.

Plane engines failed. Pilot steered plane so that it glided towards the river and landed there. Everyone survived.

Who were the people involved?

Pilot: Chesley B. "Sully" Sullenberger

155 people on board

Air traffic controllers and energency rescue services

When did it happen?

Thursday 15 January 2009

Where did it happen?

Hudson River, near La Guardia airport, New York USA

Why did it happen?

Bird strike caused both the plane's engines to fail shortly after take-off

Pilot was skilled and experienced and kept calm

More questions

Were people hurt?

How were people rescued from the river?

Are planes often damaged by birds?

Figure 1.2
Recording answers

When you are researching information, you should be asking yourself questions about the sources you use.

The '5 W's

Figure 1.3 *Using sources of information*

Earlier you met the '5 W' questions: what, who, when, where and why. These can be applied to sources of information. When doing research, key questions to ask about sources include:

- What information is this source telling me?
- Who produced this source? Was it produced by an individual person or an organisation?
- When was this source produced? Is it still up to date?
- Where is the information placed? Is it on a website? If so, which one?
- Why has this source been produced? Is it there simply to inform? Is it meant to convince me of a particular point of view?

a4: CORRECT AND COMPLETE?

IE TW E

In a group, suggest and discuss reasons why some information sources might not be correct or complete.

Primary or secondary?

Another useful question is:

- Is this a primary or secondary source?

In other words, is the person who produced the source telling you about something they experienced or found out themselves? Or are they reporting something that other people did or found out? A primary source can be very valuable because it describes first-hand experience, but it might only tell part of the story.

Biased?

PROJECT HINT

An evaluation of the sources used for your Project will help you to demonstrate a high level of achievement.

A **biased** source is one that is one-sided. Sometimes bias is accidental, if someone only tells you what they know, but they don't know everything. But sometimes it is deliberate, if someone leaves out information that they don't want you to know. To get some idea of whether a source might be biased, ask these questions:

- Is the source produced by a person or organisation that has something to gain by getting people to agree with their point of view?
- Is the source produced by someone who is in a position to know all the facts?
- Are there any obvious gaps in the information provided?

Reliable?

A **reliable** source is one that provides information that you can be pretty sure is correct. It is not easy to be certain whether a source is reliable, but these questions can be useful:

- Is the source produced by a recognised expert? Or a student? Or by someone who is just interested in the topic?
- Are experts involved in checking the information?
- Does the source have a good reputation for being reliable?

a5: EVALUATING AN INFORMATION SOURCE IE CT E

Choose a magazine article, a leaflet or a website with information on a topic that you are interested in and carry out an evaluation using the questions listed above.

1.3 You ask the questions

Producing a questionnaire

One good way to gather information for your Project is to carry out some primary research using a **questionnaire** (Figure 1.4). By asking the same set of simple questions to a large number of people, you can collect information quite quickly and easily. The answers can sometimes show interesting patterns and trends. Because you ask everybody the same questions, you can draw a definite conclusion from your research – you can say that you have found out something that is more general than just one person's answer.

PROJECT HINT

Using your own questionnaire to collect information for your Project will help you to demonstrate good research skills.

You might use a questionnaire face to face and record people's answers yourself, or you might hand out your questionnaire for people to fill in themselves. Either way, two golden rules for a good questionnaire are:

- Keep it simple.
- Try it out.

The first rule applies to all aspects of a questionnaire: questions and answers, instructions and information, and design. If your questionnaire is not simple, people will get confused and bored, and they will either stop answering or give random unhelpful answers.

Questions and answers

- Limit yourself to about seven questions at most.
- Only ask questions that directly relate to what you want to find out.

Figure 1.4
Using a questionnaire

When writing your questions, think about the sort of answers you want. The simplest questions to use are **closed questions**, meaning that people have to choose from a set of possible answers that you give them. The very simplest closed questions have 'yes' or 'no' as the only possible answers.

Sometimes you will need to ask **open questions**, which allow people to answer however they wish. Open questions can produce interesting and unexpected information, but it can be hard to group different people's answers together and draw general conclusions from them.

Avoid using **leading questions** that are designed to get the answers that you think you want. Your research will be much more interesting and reliable if you don't try to influence people's answers.

- Use closed questions at the beginning of the questionnaire.
- If you use open questions, put them at the end.
- Provide spaces or tick-boxes for the answers.

You can record answers to closed questions using tick-boxes. Provide space for written answers to open questions. About four lines is usually enough – you don't want the answers to be too long.

Instructions and information

- Make all your instructions clear and easy to follow.
- As far as possible, avoid using words people might not know.
- If you need to use technical terms, jargon or abbreviations, explain what they mean.
- Arrange your questions in a sensible order.

Design

Your questionnaire should be clear and easy to use.

- Type your questionnaire.
- Choose a font that is clear and not too small or too big.
- Use plenty of white space.
- If you use tick-boxes, line them up at the right-hand side of the sheet.

Try it out

This is the second golden rule. You can never be sure that your questionnaire is easy to use until you try it. Finding problems after you've handed out 50 copies is too late.

When you have drafted your questionnaire, try it out on a few people in your class or at home before you start your main information collection. Ask them for some feedback. If they tell you the questions are unclear, or the questionnaire is hard to follow, ask them how you could improve it. If the answers you collect are not as useful as you hoped, think how you might alter the questions, or give a different choice of tick-box answers.

Using a questionnaire

You need to make some decisions about how to use your questionnaire. Ask yourself some questions to help you decide what to do.

ab: GOOD OR BAD QUESTIONS?

CT TW E

Figure 1.5 shows parts of two questionnaires about TV viewing. In a group, discuss whether you think these are good or bad and say how they could be made better.

How many?

How many people do you want to answer your questionnaire? You need enough people to give you a reasonable amount of information, but not so many that you don't have time to deal with all their answers. Aim to get between 20 and 50 sets of answers.

Who?

Who will you ask? This will depend on what you are trying to find out. You might want to give your questionnaire only to certain groups of people (e.g. people between ages 14 and 16, or people who own dogs), or you might want to aim for balance (e.g. equal numbers of male and female) or compare equal numbers from two groups (e.g. vegetarians and meat-eaters).

Handout or face to face?

Will you hand out your questionnaire or use it face to face? Handing it out takes up less of your time, but not everyone will complete it and give it back.

(a) Part of Beth's questionnaire

1 How much TV do you watch in a week?

....

2 Which programmes do you watch?

....

....

....

....

....

....

(b) Part of Dan's questionnaire

How many hours do you watch TV each day?

less than 1 hour
1-2 hours
2-3 hours
more than 3 hours

Which sort of programmes do you watch?
(Tick all that you watch at least once per week)

Sport
News
Soap/drama (e.g. East Enders)
Factual (e.g. Horizon)
Reality (e.g Big Brother)
Comedy
Quiz/game shows (e.g. Countdown)

Figure 1.5
Good or bad questions?

a7: YOU ASK THE QUESTIONS

E TW RL SM

In a small group, design a questionnaire to find out about people's TV viewing – how much time they spend watching TV, and what sorts of programmes they watch. Follow the advice given above, then try out your questionnaire on a few people and ask for their feedback. Use the feedback to help improve your questionnaire. Finally, use the questionnaire to collect data from 20 people.

PROJECT HINT

Use the feedback from Activity 7 to help you design a good questionnaire for your Project.

1.4–1.5 Dealing with data

Displaying data

The word **data** means factual information from measurements or surveys, generally in the form of numbers. If you make measurements, or use a questionnaire, or look up numbers or measurements in some secondary source, you are collecting data.

To make good use of your data, a helpful first step is to put it all in a table with clear headings, like Table 1.1. If you collect data using a questionnaire with tick-boxes, use a separate table for each question.

Table 1.1
Data on TV viewing

Hours of TV watched each day	Number of people who watch this much TV
less than 1 hour	3
1–2 hours	16
2–3 hours	23
more than 3 hours	8

When you have your data in a table, you can sometimes see patterns and trends. These are even easier to see if you display your data using a chart. You, and everyone else, can see any patterns at a glance.

Use a computer package, such as Excel, to help you make charts. Bar and column charts are best when the answers involve numbers that go from small to large as in Table 1.1 (0–1 hours, 1–2 hours and so on). Figure 1.6 is a chart of data from Table 1.1 and it clearly shows an 'up-and-down' pattern in the data. Most people in the survey watched 1–3 hours of TV a day, and only a few watch more than this or less.

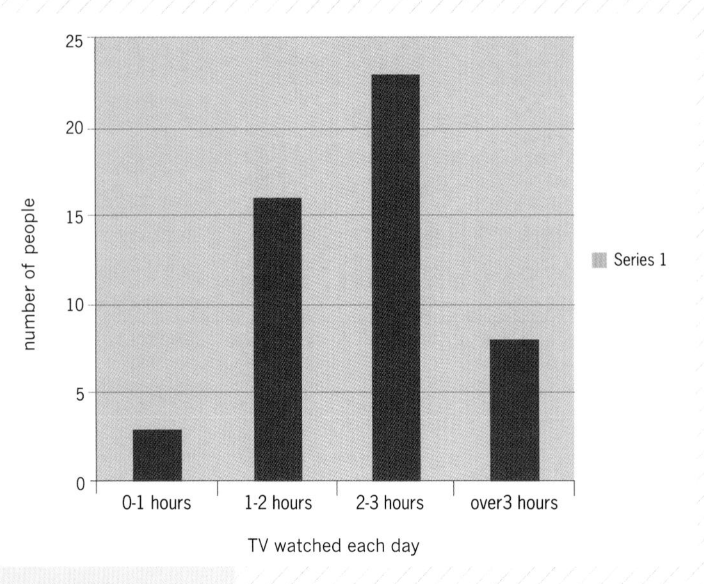

Figure 1.6
Column chart displaying the data from Table 1.1

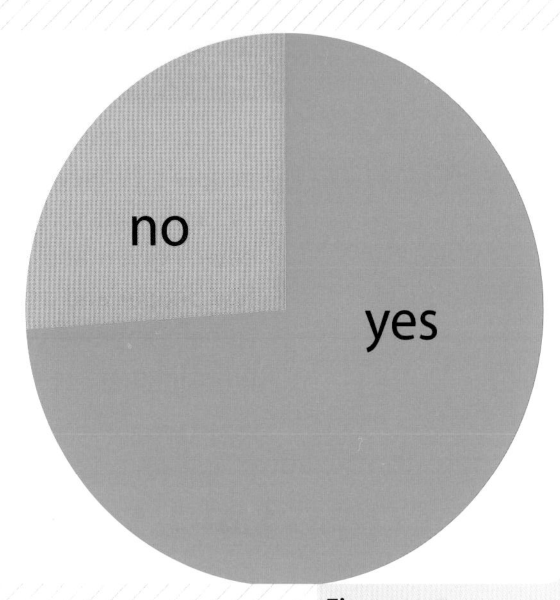

Figure 1.7
Pie chart to show whether people in a survey watch satellite TV

If your data shows that a fixed number of people (or things) are divided between several groups, you can use a pie chart. This is a good way to display data from a question where each person chooses just one answer. For example, when 50 people were asked whether they watch satellite TV, 37 said yes and 13 said no. Their answers are displayed in Figure 1.7.

PROJECT HINT

Using tables and charts in your Project will help you demonstrate good communication skills.

Warning: Do not use a pie chart if people can choose more than one answer. Some people will be in more than one group. For example, when 50 people were asked what type of TV programmes they watched, they were allowed to tick as many boxes as they liked (Table 1.2). To display data from that sort of question, it is best to use a bar chart or column chart, with the size of each group shown by the length of a different bar or column.

Type of programme	Number of people who watch
news	41
sports	33
.... (several types omitted) ...	...
lifestyle	13
factual	12

Table 1.2
What sorts of TV programmes do you watch?

Remember: you do not have to use the same sort of chart for all your questions. Choose the best sort of chart each time.

a8: USING CHARTS

Practise using bar/column charts and pie charts. Look at the data you collected in Activity 7, and discuss in a group how to display the data. Use Excel to draw the charts.

On average

Sometimes it is sensible to calculate an average from your data. For example, if you measure the height of four people and get the results 1.45 m, 1.67 m, 1.54 m and 1.45 m, the average is:

$$(1.45 \text{ m} + 1.67 \text{ m} + 1.54 \text{ m} + 1.45 \text{ m}) \div 4 = 1.53 \text{ m (2 d.p.)}$$

Sometimes you need to think a bit before you do the calculation. Suppose you want to use data from Table 1.1 to find the average length of time that people watch TV. You need to think how to use numbers such as '1–2 hours' or 'over 3 hours'. It is probably sensible to use '1.5 hours' instead of '1–2 hours', and so on, then for 'over 3 hours' you might guess that 4 hours is a sensible amount of time. See Table 1.3.

Hours of TV watched each day	Number of hours used to calculate average	Number of people who watch this much TV
less than 1 hour	0.5	3
1–2 hours	1.5	16
2–3 hours	2.5	23
more than 3 hours	4.0	8

Table 1.3
Data on TV viewing from Table 1.1

To find the average, you then calculate:

$$(3 \times 0.5 \text{ hours} + 16 \times 1.5 \text{ hours} + 23 \times 2.5 \text{ hours} + 8 \times 4.0 \text{ hours}) \div 50 = 2.3 \text{ hours.}$$

You could then sum up your results by saying that, on average, the people surveyed watched 2.3 hours of TV each day.

But beware: an average does not always give a sensible answer. Table 1.4 shows people's answers to the question 'How many TV sets are there in your home?'

Table 1.4
How many TV sets are there in your home?

Number of TV sets	Number of homes with this number of TV sets
0	1
1	26
2	18
3	4
4	1
5 or more	0

The average number of TV sets is 1.56. But that doesn't mean that any home actually has 1.56 TV sets. It would be better to describe the data in Table 1.3 by saying that that just over half of the homes (26 out of 50) had one TV set, over a third had two sets, and the vast majority (44 out of 50) had either one or two sets.

a9: USING AVERAGES

In your group, look at your data from Activity 7, discuss whether it is sensible to calculate any averages, then carry out the calculations. Decide whether you could use other ways to sum up the data.

Conclusions and significance

As well as displaying your data in charts you need to state your **conclusions** – in other words, say what you have found out from your data.

A good researcher will be able to discuss the **significance** of their conclusions, which means saying how confident the researcher is in the reliability and correctness of the data used. Two things that indicate the significance of a conclusion based on a collection of data are the amount of data (the number of measurements, samples or answers) and the range of the results. Significance will also be affected if your collection of data has been biased in some way. A discussion of significance might include all three of these points.

> **PROJECT HINT**
>
> A discussion of the significance of your Project's conclusions will help you to demonstrate a high level of achievement.

Bias

If you think your data collection has been biased in some way, you need to point this out when you discuss the significance of your conclusion.

For example, suppose you were researching people's TV viewing, and all the people you asked were males in the age range 25 to 40. You would need to say that your conclusions applied only to 25 to 40-year-old males, not to people in general.

Amount of data

In general, the more data you have, the more significant your conclusion. When discussing your conclusions, you need to say how much data you collected.

Suppose you asked just three people what sort of TV programmes they watched and the only one they all ticked was 'sport'. Your conclusion might be that sport was the most popular sort of TV programme. Then suppose you asked 50 people and the most popular was 'news', watched by 41 people, followed by 'sport', watched by 33 people (Table 1.2).

A conclusion based on just three people is not very significant. It is not reliable and really doesn't mean much. If you asked another three people you would be quite likely to get a different answer. But a conclusion based on 50 people is more significant; it is quite likely that if you included more from the same group of people you would get similar results.

Range

The range or 'spread' in your data relates to the significance of your conclusions and you should include this in your discussion.

For example, look at Table 1.2 where the types of programmes are listed in order of popularity. There is quite a big difference between 'news' and 'sports', so you can say that 'news' is significantly the most popular type of programme. But there is only a very small difference between 'factual' and 'lifestyle', so you cannot say that 'factual' is significantly the least popular.

Range is also useful if you have calculated an average. In the example of time spent watching TV, in Tables 1.1 and 1.3 and Figure 1.6, you can say that the average is 2.3 hours, and most people are in the range 1 to 3 hours. If you asked another 50 people, you might not get exactly the same average, but it would probably still be in the range 1 to 3 hours.

a10: CONCLUSIONS AND SIGNIFICANCE

IE TW RL E M

In your group, look at your results from Activity 7. Discuss your conclusions and their significance.

2 Developing your skills and ideas

2.1 Issues in the making

Issues in the making

An important part of your Project is that you should think about some of the issues involved. When you write a report, or tell people about your Project, you should say something about the issues and how you have addressed them. There might be practical issues, so that you have to develop some practical or problem-solving skills, or there might be issues that you can explore in some written work. The sorts of issues will partly depend on the sort of Project you are doing.

An **artefact** is a general name for something that is designed and made (Figure 2.1). If you will be making an artefact for your Project, it is a good idea to study some that other people have made. When studying an artefact, it is useful to ask some questions about it. They are like the '5 W' questions that you use when gathering information from other sources, plus a sixth question: 'How?'

Figure 2.1
An artefact

- *What* is it? *What* is it made with?
- *Who* made it? *Who* was it made for?
- *When* was it made?
- *Where* was it made? *Where* is it now?
- *Why* was it made?
- *How* was it made?

a11: LOOKING AT ARTEFACTS E  

Study an artefact that someone else has made and try to answer the '5 W + H' questions.

COURSE REF.

For more on the '5 W' questions see Lesson 1.1.

PROJECT SPRINGBOARD

Studying artefacts made by other people might give you some ideas for your own Project.

Asking the '5 W + H' questions about your own artefact will help you see the issues involved. You need to ask 'What will it be? When will it be made?' and so on. The answers will help you write a **design brief** for your Project. For developing your ideas and skills, the following three sets of questions are important.

Why make it? Who is it for?

Early on, you need to think and explain why you are making your artefact.

- Are you making something for decoration, or for practical use?
- Is it intended to solve a problem?
- Is it for a particular person, or group of people?

What is it made with?

Think about what you use to make your artefact. Explore the different media and materials available for your work. Try out different ones, decide which to use and explain why you chose them. For example, if you are making an object, think about the different materials available and whether they are suitable:

- Are the materials easy to work with?
- What do they look like?
- Will they wear out quickly?
- Are they expensive?
- Where do they come from? Do they have to be transported from far away?

If you are making something on a computer (such as a website), think about the different software packages that you might use.

How is it made?

When you are making your artefact, you will probably have to develop some new skills. You also need to think about the processes and technology. Try different approaches, decide how best to make your artefact, and explain why you did it that way.

On site

Before you choose your own project topic, look at how other people have made things and developed their skills. This will help you to make a good choice of topic and to plan your own work.

a12: ON SITE E ICT IE CT RL

Read the description of a website Project. Answer these questions and discuss how Dev used his Project to develop his skills and ideas.

1. Why did Dev make the new web pages?
2. Who were the pages made for?
3. What did he use to make them?
4. What were the issues that Dev had to address?

PROJECT SPRINGBOARD

A real-life issue can be a good starting point for a Project.

For his Project, Dev redesigned some pages on his sports club website to make it easier for people to find out about events. He first looked at the old pages and made a checklist of features that made them easy or difficult to use. Then he looked at a site belonging to another club and compared the two. Dev found that there were rules about making web pages accessible to people with dyslexia. This made him rethink some of his ideas about design.

Next he explored three different computer software packages that could be used to make web pages. To do this, he needed to learn some new computing skills. He listed the advantages and disadvantages of the packages before making his choice.

Finally he produced his new pages. He used his checklist to evaluate the pages, and asked for comments from his tutor, the club organisers, and other people in the club.

2.2 In the event

In the event

Your Project might involve an event, such as a drama performance or a group visit to a place of interest (Figure 2.2). To help you think about and plan your own event, study some that other people have organised. It is useful to ask

some questions based on the '5 W' questions that you use for gathering information, plus the extra question, 'How?'

- *What* happened?
- *Who* organised it? *Who* was it for?
- *When* did it happen?
- *Where* did it happen?
- *Why* was it organised?
- *How* was it organised?

a13: THINKING ABOUT EVENTS

E IE CT

Think about an event that you have been to, and try to answer the '5 W + H' questions.

Asking the '5 W + H' questions about your own planned event will help you see the issues involved. You will probably answer the question 'What is it?' on your Project Proposal Form. For developing your ideas and skills, the following sets of questions are important.

Why organise it?

- Is your event something just for people to enjoy?
- Do you want people to learn something from your event? Or to change their ideas?
- What do you hope to learn from the event?

Figure 2.2
An event

Who is it for?

- Who will take part in your event?
- Is there an audience? Who are they?
- Does anyone have special needs? How will you help them take part?

When and where will it happen?

- Do you need to book a venue?
- Do you need to organise transport?
- Do you need to arrange rehearsals? Where and when will they happen?

How will it be organised?

- Do you need to write to, phone or text other people to help arrange your event?
- Do you need to advertise your event? How will you do this?

For all ages

Before you decide on your own project topic, have a look at how other people have organised events and developed their skills. This will help you to make a good choice of topic and to plan your own work.

a14: FOR ALL AGES

Read the description of a Project to organise an event. Answer these questions and discuss how Mel used the Project to develop her skills and ideas.

- Who was the audience?
- What skills did Mel have to learn?
- What information sources did she use?
- What were the issues that Mel had to address?

PROJECT HINT

If you work on a group Project, make sure your own role is clear.

PROJECT HINT

Learning a new skill will help you demonstrate a high level of achievement in your Project.

For her Project, Mel worked in a group of six to put on a show with music for the rest of their class. The class went on a visit to theatre and took part in a workshop with musicians.

Their teacher suggested that Mel's group could explore the question 'how do people of different ages respond to music?' In a group meeting, they planned six parts for the performance, each about 5 minutes long. Each part focused on a different age. The group agreed that each part should include a mime, dance or a spoken scene, some images projected onto a screen, and some music. Each person had to organise one part and choose the music and images, and they would all take part in all the scenes. Other tasks were divided up so that one person made a poster, one designed the programme, and so on.

Mel's part was about old people. Her teacher gave her some magazine articles about music and drama and Mel used these to help her research for her part of the show. She talked to her gran about the music she liked, and visited an old people's day centre to see how music was used in exercise classes and for entertainment.

She learned how to record and edit clips for a CD. She recorded some music tracks and made a CD that she played to 20 people at the day centre, then she gave them a questionnaire asking which tracks they liked and why. This helped her choose the tracks for her part of the show. Mel's research also gave her some ideas for images. She learned how to paste images from websites into PowerPoint and set up a slideshow.

Mel devised a mime based on her visits to the day centre, and arranged rehearsals with the rest of the group. She also took part in rehearsals for the other scenes. Finally the whole group performed their show, which they called 'music for all ages'.

2.3 What's the answer?

What's the answer?

If you are doing a written Project, a good way to give your work focus is to start with a question. Good project questions are often the sort that ask, 'What should be done about ...? or 'Is it right that ...?' Your Project is then about exploring the issues and answering the question.

Issues about what is right, or what is good, belong to the subject known as **ethics**. Ethics is all about how we ought to live. Ethical issues include: What is wrong with lying? Should we ever break the law? Should parents have the right to expect their children to follow a particular religion? Is it right to use animals to test new cosmetic products? What rights should a 16-year-old have? How should we trade with developing countries?

When you are exploring a question for your Project, think about it in two ways.

- *What* do you think? *What* do you believe is the answer to your question?
- *Why* do you think that? *Why* do you believe that is the answer?

To deal with these questions, you will need to develop your thinking skills.

What do you think?

You might already have strong views about your question before you start. Or maybe you can see several sides and you are not sure what is the best answer. Either way, by the time you have done some work on your Project, you should aim to come up with your own definite **point of view**.

Why do you think that?

You might have a strong point of view, and perhaps the right answer to your question seems obvious to you, but not everybody will agree. Other people will have a different point of view. You need to give your **reasons**. That is, explain carefully why you think your point of view is the best.

To help you work out and explain your reasons, you need to do some research. This will be a big part of your Project. Try to find out the main **facts** that relate to your question, and what other people have said or written about their points of view on your question.

Your research will help you to think more clearly about your point of view. You will probably find that it helps you to make up – or even change – your mind. If you explain your reasons well, you might persuade other people to agree with you.

PROJECT SPRINGBOARD

A question about using animals in research could be a good one to explore in a written Project.

a15: WHAT DO YOU THINK? WHY? TW CT RL 

Should we use pig hearts (Figure 2.3) for human transplants?

List some reasons why you think pig hearts should, or should not, be used for human transplants. Then in a small group, compare your ideas with other people.

In your group, list the facts that you would need to research if you were doing a Project on this question.

Figure 2.3
Pig

Junk advertising

Before you decide you own Project topic, look at the ways other people have researched their Projects and developed their skills. This will help you to make a good choice of topic and to plan your own work.

a16: JUNK ADVERTISING   

Read the description of a Project that explored an ethical question. Answer these questions and discuss how Zak used the Project to develop his skills and ideas.

- What was Zak's point of view when he started?
- What primary and secondary research did he do?
- What were his reasons for changing his point of view?

Zak heard that some health experts wanted to stop 'junk foods' (unhealthy foods such as burgers, crisps and sweets, Figure 2.4) being advertised on children's TV. For his Project, Zak researched the question 'Should junk food advertising be banned from children's TV?'

Zak started off thinking the ads should not be banned. He thought that children would buy crisps and sweets anyway, and they should be able to choose the food they enjoy eating. He thought their parents would stop them eating too much bad food. He also thought that shopkeepers would suffer if children did not buy so many sweets and crisps.

In their PSHE lessons, Zak's class had learned how diet affects health. For his Project, Zak used information from biology books to find out more about how fat, sugar and salt affect health.

Zak gave a questionnaire to a class of young children to find out what snack foods they bought and whether they took any notice of TV advertisements. He also gave a questionnaire to some parents to find out their views on their children's eating.

Zak used websites to find the views of health experts and the reasons why they wanted to ban the advertisements. He also found some information on the amount of sweets and crisps sold in the UK and the profits made by manufacturers and shops.

During his Project, Zak changed his mind about banning the advertisements. He found that there were reasons for and against the ban and he had to decide which were best. He found this quite hard. He thought carefully about what might happen if the advertisements were banned or if they were not.

In his written report Zak explained that eating unhealthy food when very young can cause health problems later, and that doctors and dentists were worried about young children eating too much junk food. He also explained that children did seem to want junk food because they had seen advertisements, and their parents found it difficult to stop them. He thought it was wrong that manufacturers made large profits from selling unhealthy food, and that it would not matter too much if they sold less.

Figure 2.4
Junk food

PROJECT SPRINGBOARD

A question about a health issue could be a good starting point for a written Project. Another good starting point could be a question about advertising.

PROJECT HINT

Use your planner to help you write your Project Activity Log.

2.4 Thinking skills

Reasons

Your Project will involve deciding to do things in a certain way, or deciding on a particular point of view, and you should try to explain why you made those decisions. In a written Project, you can take this a step further: when you are setting out the reasons for your point of view, try to say something about the different types of reasons that you are using. In other words, think about your ways of thinking.

PROJECT HINT

Thinking about thinking is quite an advanced skill. Commenting on your reasons will help you demonstrate a high level of achievement.

Look back at Activity 15, where you thought about using pig hearts in transplants and gave reasons for your point of view. You can probably list your group's reasons under the following headings.

Outcomes

Thinking about the **outcome** is one way to decide whether or not something should be done. For example, if you think that pig hearts should be used in transplants because more people will be helped to live a healthy life, then your reason is based on the outcome.

Rights

Another way of thinking involves the idea of **rights**. For example, you might be against the idea of using pig hearts because you think that animals have the right not to be killed and used to benefit humans. On the other hand, you might think that pig hearts should be used because humans have rights to a healthy life, and that human rights are more important than animal rights.

Figure 2.5 *Religious texts set out rules for how to behave*

Religious rules

For many people, **religious rules** (Figure 2.5) set out what is right and wrong. If you have a religious faith, that probably affects your views on transplants. Some religions, such as Buddhism, are against killing animals. Others, such as Islam and Judaism, regard pigs as unclean so would not want pig hearts to be placed inside people.

a17: REASONS

TW

Look back at Activity 16. Working in a small group, list Zak's reasons for thinking that junk food advertisements should, or should not, be banned. Then decide whether each reason is based on outcomes, rights or religious rules.

To help your thinking, ask yourself these questions.

- Would a ban make more people happy, or less happy?
- Would a ban make more people healthy, or less healthy?
- Do you think young children have a right to choose what they eat?
- Do you think parents have a right to decide what their children eat?

Reasons and objections

When you have come to a point of view on a question, think how you might persuade other people to agree with you. If you set out your reasons clearly and explain your thinking, then you might hope that everyone else will see the sense and agree that you are right. But it is not always like that. People have their own points of view and reasons for disagreeing with you. To make a really strong **argument** for your point of view, you need to think about the **objections** that people might have to your reasons, and think how you will respond to them.

For example, in Zak's Project about advertising, he said that it was wrong for manufacturers to make large profits from selling unhealthy food. His friend Mik objected that 'if manufacturers make less money, then their workers will lose their jobs, so it's wrong to ban the advertising'. Zak's response was that 'the manufacturers should make more healthy foods instead, so people are not harmed by eating them and the manufacturers can still employ the same number of workers'.

PROJECT HINT

Setting out an argument using reasons and objections is an advanced thinking skill. If you can do this in your Project, you will be demonstrating a high level of achievement.

a18: OBJECTIONS

TW

Look back at Activities 15 and 16. Working with a partner, try to think of objections to the reasons for or against using pig hearts or banning junk food advertising. Then discuss how someone might respond to each objection.

3 Planning your Project

3.1 Choosing your Project

When you have learned some useful skills and looked at some examples of other Projects, you will be ready to start work on your own Project. For any Project at Level 1 or 2, you will need to:

- choose a suitable topic
- identify a question or a brief that relates to a definite objective
- plan how you will reach your objective
- carry out some research using suitable techniques
- reach your intended outcome using suitable tools and techniques safely
- communicate the outcome of your project
- review your own learning and performance.

In this chapter, we will deal with the first three of these points.

Topic and objective

You might have your own ideas about project topics, or your teacher/tutor might suggest some. Your Project will work best if it is about something that matters to you, so try to choose a topic that you care about. It is good if your Project can explore issues relating to your particular interests, and perhaps to your future work or study.

Your Project will also work best if you choose a question to research, or have a clear design brief. It is easier to research if you have a clear question that you are trying to answer.

Think about the work you will do for your Project. A good Project will help you build up your skills and learn more about your topic.

Also think about the time you will spend on your Project. Altogether you will need to allow about 40 hours – which is quite a long time.

Spend time thinking about your **objective** – in other words, what you want to achieve. The best Projects have a very clear objective. If you know what you are trying to do, then you can focus your work.

All Projects should include some research, so check that there are some information sources that you can use.

COURSE REF.

See Lesson 1.1 for some suggestions about information sources.

Sal hoped one day to work for an environmental charity, and she wanted to do her Project on the environment. But that is a very broad topic, and Sal was unsure where to start. She talked to her teacher about how to focus her Project.

In Sal's town, the council wanted to cut down the amount of waste going into landfill sites (Figure 3.1). A letter in the local paper said there was a big problem with young people dropping drinks cartons and food wrappings in the streets. After talking with her teacher, Sal decided on a research question: 'How can young people be persuaded to recycle packaging waste?'

The question gave Sal's Project work a clear focus. She wrote a questionnaire and gave it to people aged 14 to 18, asking about their own behaviour and views. She analysed their responses and drew charts to summarise them.

She also carried out some secondary research using websites and newspapers. This helped her to learn about what happens to recycled materials, the cost of recycling, and how different countries organise the collection of waste to be recycled.

At the end of her Project, Sal was able to make some clear statements about young people's views on packaging, waste and recycling, and she was able to state her own point of view on how young people might be encouraged to recycle more. She felt that her work had helped her to understand some of the issues.

Figure 3.1
A landfill site

a19: TOPIC AND OBJECTIVE

E RL SM

Spend some time thinking about possible topics for your project work. Talk about your ideas with your teacher/tutor. Then decide on your objective for your Project.

Project proposal

Once you have some idea about the topic of your Project, and have thought about your objective, you will need to write a Project proposal.

Do not rush this important stage. It is best to spend time at the start thinking carefully about what you want to do. Otherwise you might jump in and find later that your objective is vague or unrealistic, or simply that you lose interest in your Project.

Title, objective and responsibilities

It is best if your title is in the form of a question.

For the objective, say what you want to achieve in your Project.

If you are working on a group Project, you need to say what your role is.

If you are going to make an artefact, write a **design brief** – a single sentence saying 'in a nutshell' what your Project will be.

Reasons

You need to say why you have chosen this Project. Just saying 'because it is part of my course' is a weak reason. Try to give reasons that are personal to you. For example, the topic might link to issues that affect you, your family or friends, or to your plans for further study or a career. Or perhaps you want to use your Project to develop some new skills.

Activities and timescales

This needs quite a lot of thought. Forty hours works out at about two or three lessons a week, plus homework time, for the whole of one term. You need to have some idea of how you will divide up the time, otherwise there is a risk that you either try to do too much and run out of time, or run out of ideas and end up not doing very much.

Resources

Try to be definite here. It is easy just to say 'books and Internet' but make sure there are some useful sources that you can easily lay your hands on. It is a good idea to spend a bit of time checking this before you write your final proposal.

COURSE REF.

Lesson 3.2 gives you some advice about planning your time.

a20: PROJECT PROPOSAL

Write a proposal for your Project. Discuss your proposal with your teacher/tutor and change it as necessary before handing it in.

3.2 Planning your time

One step at a time

A good plan will help you do a good Project. The chart in Figure 3.2 shows the main stages in a Project. Different sorts of Projects will need different things. For example, while some people are rehearsing for an event, others might be collecting data using a questionnaire. You will need to make your own plan for your own Project, and you need to think how long each stage will take.

To plan a Project, you need to break it down into smaller tasks – a bite-sized approach. This will:

- help you to think through the whole Project in outline
- make the Project more manageable and less daunting
- focus your attention on each task in a sensible order.

Identify some key **milestones** – tasks that you will need to finish before going on to the next stage of your Project. Reaching your milestones will show that you have made progress towards your objective. Find out key dates from your teacher/tutor. You might be asked to finish certain tasks by a given date or perhaps to hand in some work.

For each task, think how long it might take. This is difficult without actually doing it, but start by thinking about other things that you have done that were a bit similar.

Think about the order of doing things. In most Projects there are things that need to be done near the beginning (such as trying out a questionnaire) and others that can only be done near the end (such as holding a dress rehearsal for a performance).

Write down all the tasks and milestones for your Project and put them on a **timeline**. To help you do this, you could write each task on a Post-it sticker and arrange them in a sensible order.

COURSE REF.

A well-thought-out plan will help you demonstrate good organisational skills.

Decide on your topic and your objective. Write your project title as a question. Fill in your Project Proposal Form. Write a plan for your project work. Start keeping an Activity Log.		
Find some good secondary sources of information		
Decide how you will gather primary data	Write your design brief	Hold a meeting to plan your event
Make up a questionnaire and test it on 10 people Rewrite it if you need to Give out your questionnaire	Make models, sketches, photographs, etc.	Arrange the venue for your event Hold progress meetings Take part in workshops and reshearsals
Carry on with your project: researching secondary information exploring issues collecting primary data designing and making your object developing and rehearsing your event keeping your Activity Log up to date.		
Analyse your data State your conclusion	Produce the final version of your object	Take part in your event
Produce a record of your work (e.g. written report, sketch book, etc.) Make sure your Activity Log is complete		
Do a presentation of your project		
Evaluate your project (say what you learned, what went well, and what you would do differently if you did it again)		

Figure 3.2
Outline plan of a Project

At this stage you cannot know all the problems that might crop up, so build some extra time into your plan in case you need it.

Making an artefact

If you are making something (Figure 3.3), you will need to go through the stages listed in Table 3.1. You will probably need to spend about one quarter of your time on analysis and research, one quarter on ideas and development, and one third on production planning and making your final artefact. Use the rest of the time for testing and evaluation.

Figure 3.3
Making an artefact

Brief	Write a single sentence describing your Project 'in a nutshell'.
Analysis and research	Refine the brief and describe the task in more detail. Research how other people have worked to a similar brief.
Specification	Make a detailed list of points the artefact should satisfy.
Ideas and development	Explore and try out different approaches. Decide on the approach you will take.
Production plan	Make a detailed plan showing the materials, techniques and processes you will use. Include a timescale.
Realisation	Make the artefact.
Testing and review	A report of your work. Did it meet the specification? How could it be improved?

Table 3.1
Stages in desiging and making an artefact

COURSE REF.

Chapter 4 will give you some more guidance on each stage.

Event

Table 3.2 lists stages in a group performance project (Figure 3.4). You will have to spend some time working with the rest of your group and some time working on your own part. You will probably need to spend about one third of your time on research and analysis of your own part of the Project and about one third exploring and trying out different approaches. About one third of your time will probably be spent on group meetings and rehearsals.

Figure 3.4
Planning a group performance Project

If you are working on a group event that is not a performance, you can use Table 3.2 as a starting point but think how to change it to suit your own Project.

Group briefing	Write a single sentence describing your group Project 'in a nutshell'. Agree each person's contribution.
Analysis and research	Describe your own part of the Project in more detail. Carry out research that relates to your own part.
Group meetings	Hold workshops and brainstorming sessions to develop ideas. Share information about work in progress.
Ideas and development	Explore and try out different approaches.
Group rehearsals	Agree the details of your performance. Plan and take part in rehearsals.
Performance	The actual performance.
Review	A report of your work. Did you do what you set out to do? How could your part be improved?

Table 3.2
Stages in a group performance Project

Written Project

For a written Project, think about your report right from the start. This will help you to plan your Project work. It is best to organise your report into sections as shown in Table 3.3. You can then work on one section at a time and write each one up as you go along. This is much better than leaving it all to the end. Spend about one third of your time on the research section, almost half your time on discussion, and the rest on the introduction and review.

Table 3.3
Structure for a written Project

Introduction	Explanation of your research question Reasons why you chose your topic
Research	The information you have found References Comments on your sources of information*
Discussion	Your answer to your research question Your reasons for your answer Your comments on other possible answers
Review	How your ideas and skills have developed What you have learned from your Project What worked well and what did not What you would do differently next time* What else you would do if you had more time
Bibliography	List of exactly where you found your secondary information

*Only needed for Level 2

a21: ONE STEP AT A TIME

E RL SM

Decide what the main stages of your Project are. Use Figure 3.2 and Tables 3.1, 3.2 and 3.3 to help you get started. Ask your teacher/tutor for the key dates.

Write your tasks and milestones on Post-it stickers and arrange them into a timeline.

COURSE REF.

Chapter 4 will give you some advice on each section.

Project planner

Use your timeline to start your project planner. Table 3.4 shows an example. The project planner will help you to keep up to date with your work. It will also help you at the end of your Project when you look back over your work.

Table 3.4
Project planner

Week	Date	What I plan to do	What I actually did
1			
2			
3			

a22: PROJECT PLANNER

E RL SM

Using your timeline from Activity 21, fill in the left-hand and middle columns of your project planner.

Keep your project planner in a safe place, e.g. in the front of your Project file or above your desk. Look at your chart at the start of each week so that you know what to do. At the end of each week make a note of what you actually did.

If you need to change your plan as you go along, make a note of what you change and why. Unless you need a *completely* new plan, do this by neatly crossing out and adding notes. You will then have a record of how your work developed. This will be very useful when you write up and evaluate your Project.

PROJECT HINT

A well-kept project planner will help you demonstrate good organisational skills and will help you to review your progress.

4 Carrying out your Project

4.1 Getting started

Record keeping

Now you have chosen your Project and planned your work, you are ready to start. One golden rule for Project work is:

- Keep your records up to date.

For all types of Project you will be finding out information and making notes. Keep these safely in a file or a folder (Figure 4.1). If you are using a computer, put all your project work in a folder and make a back-up copy at least once a week.

Figure 4.1
Keep all your notes and information safely

A box, cupboard or tray will be useful for storage if your Project involves anything other than paper-based or computer work.

If you are making an artefact, keep all your photographs, models or sketches together. Label and date them so that you can use them later to help tell the story of your Project.

For an event, think about using photos, audio recordings and video clips to record your progress. Label and date them and keep them together.

Keeping a good record will help demonstrate your skill in managing your Project work.

a23: RECORD KEEPING SM

Get together all the things you think you will need to keep a record of your Project work. Label all your files, boxes and so on with your name and your Project title.

Start writing

Another golden rule for Project work is:

- Write up as you go along.

In a written Project, your report will be the main outcome of your work. Projects leading to events or artefacts still need a written report, but it will be shorter. It is helpful to organise your report as shown in Table 4.1 so that each section focuses on a different aspect of your work. The suggested lengths are only approximate, and will vary according to the sort of Project you are doing.

Table 4.1 *Structure and length of a project report*

Section	Contents	Approximate length: Level 1		Approximate length: Level 2	
		written Project	artefact or event	written Project	artefact or event
Introduction	Explanation of your Project topic/question and objective, with reasons for choosing your Project	50–150 words	50–100 words	80–350 words	80–250 words
Research	The information you have found, with references Comments on sources*	200–600 words	100–300 words	300–900 words	120–350 words
Development/ discussion	Description of media, materials, processes and technology used Account of changes or improvements Answers to your question, and your point of view with reasons	300–700 words	100–500 words	300–1000 words	120–500 words
Review/ conclusion/ evaluation	Explanation of how your ideas and skills have developed, what worked well and what did not, what you have learned in the Project and how you would extend your Project What you would do differently another time*	70–150 words	50–200 words	120–350 words	100–300 words
Bibliography	List of exactly where you got your information from				

* Only needed at Level 2

The best place to start writing is the Introduction, because it is based on your Project proposal, which you have already written in Activity 20. You can draft this section before you do any other work for your Project, and come back to it later if you need to change it. Your Introduction should have two main parts.

Project topic or question and objective

Write down what you intend to do. Later, you might need to change this to say what you actually did.

Reasons

Explain why you have chosen this Project. This will probably be the main part of your introduction.

COURSE REF.

For more on primary and secondary research see Chapter 1 of this Guide.

a24: DRAFT INTRODUCTION

Write a draft of the Introduction section for your report. Base it on your Project Proposal Form. Keep it in a safe place so that you can return to it later.

PROJECT HINT

By keeping records up to date, writing up as you go along, you will demonstrate skills in managing, developing and realising your Project work.

4.2 Background research

It is best to start the main work on your Project with some background research. This means doing some secondary research (Figure 4.2) and writing some of the Research section of your report. The skills you developed in Chapter 1 of this Guide will help with this section, and the work you do here will contribute to the rest of your Project.

Figure 4.2 *Gathering information*

Use Table 4.2 to help you plan this part of your Project. When you are researching information, there is another golden rule for Project work:

- Focus on your Project objective.

Keep asking yourself: 'How does this relate to my Project topic? How will it help me meet my objective?' If something does not clearly link to your Project, don't spend time on it.

Project topic or question	
What will you try to find out? Think about the 'story' behind your Project, key people, events and ideas.	
What sources will you use? Where will you look? Think about libraries, museums, websites, people worth talking to.	
What will you do? Collecting materials, note-taking, building bibliography, putting together research review, editing, commenting on sources, further research.	
Target date when you aim to finish this research	

Week (date)	Actions

Table 4.2
Planning your background research

PROJECT HINT

Keeping a clear focus relates to your use of resources and will help you develop and realise your Project work.

As you find information, remember the golden rules:

- Keep your records up to date.
- Write up as you go along.

Use the '5 W' questions to help you summarise the information you find, and fill in a separate Research Record Sheet for each source you use. Then when you have looked at several sources, you can start to sort the sheets into a sensible order and put them together to help you write your Research section.

COURSE REF.

For more on the '5 W' questions and Research Record Sheets see Lesson 1.1.

The Research section is a summary of the background to your Project and includes an account of other people's work that relates to your topic. A good Research section should tell a clear 'story'. You can only really do this, however, after you have looked at several sources and found out what they say.

As far as possible, put the information in your own words rather than copying straight from the source. In some types of Project you will probably include photographs or sketches to help set out the background to your Project.

a2 5: PLANNING YOUR SECONDARY RESEARCH

Look back at your Project Proposal Form and project planner. Use them to help you plan your secondary research and fill in Table 4.2.

a2 6: STARTING THE RESEARCH SECTION

Choose *two* secondary information sources that you have used and describe how they help with your Project.

Later you can build on this work to write part of the Research section of your report.

PROJECT HINT

By focusing your work and keeping up to date with your records and writing, you will demonstrate your ability to manage, develop and realise your Project work.

COURSE REF.

For advice on designing and using questionnaires, see Lesson 1.3 of this Guide.

4.3 Primary research

When you have done some secondary research, you should start planning any primary research that you intend to do. Use Table 4.3 to help with this and remember the golden rules of Project work:

- Keep your records up to date.
- Write up as you go along.
- Focus on your project objective.

Table 4.3
Planning your primary research

Project topic or question	
What will you try to find out? Think about the information you need. Decide if you can make measurements and observations or use a questionnaire to help.	
What will you do? Drafting a trial questionnaire, getting feedback, carrying out the main information collection Setting up an experiment and making measurements Interviewing people Collecting information from fieldwork	
Target date when you aim to finish this research	
Week (date)	Actions

a27: PLANNING YOUR PRIMARY RESEARCH

CT

Use your Project Proposal Form and project planner to help you plan your primary research and fill in Table 4.3.

E

COURSE REF.

For advice on designing and using questionnaires see Lesson 1.3.

When you write up your primary research make sure you include the following.

If you used a questionnaire

- a copy of your questionnaire
- information about who you gave it to (number of people and a general description, e.g. '25 girls and 25 boys aged 14–16').

If you did any experiments

- details of any equipment you used (include diagrams or photographs)
- a description of your method.

If you made records of observations or interviews

- details of how you collected the information.

For all types of primary research

- the date(s) and place(s) where you did the research
- graphs and charts showing your data
- an account of how you analysed the data
- a statement of your results.

4.4 Writing

Writing well

Some of the marks for your Project will be for the quality of your written work. This is most important for written Projects but applies to other types too.

COURSE REF.

For advice on displaying and analysing data see Lessons 1.4 and 1.5.

Steps to help you write well

- *List* the points you want to make. Brainstorm all ideas and facts in any order.
- *Organise* them into a sensible order.
- Write a sentence to *introduce* the topic.
- Write a *sentence* for each point from your list.
- Then for each point, expand by writing a *paragraph* giving examples and explanations.
- Finish each paragraph with a sentence to *connect* it to the next paragraph.
- *End* by summing up what you have written.
- Finally, *read* your work and check that it makes sense and that your spelling and grammar are correct. Reading aloud helps; some computers have a program that will read what's on the screen.

Use the nonsense word LOISPaCER to help you remember these steps: **L**ist, **O**rganise, **I**ntroduce, **S**entence, **Pa**ragraph, **C**onnect, **E**nd, **R**ead.

a28: WRITING WELL

Use the LOISPaCER steps to write a short paragraph about a topic that interest you.

Proofreading

The final checking stage is called **proofreading**. This is where you go back and double-check that your work makes sense and your spelling, punctuation and grammar are correct. You can use a computer spell-check to help, but don't rely on it completely. Some people read backwards through thier writing word by word. A spell-check will pick up any nonsense spellings but it won't help if you have used the wrong word, or be able to tell you whether your work makes sense overall. Here is a list of questions to ask yourself when proofreading:

- Have I checked carefully for misspellings?
- Have I checked carefully for the proper use of punctuation, speech and question marks?

- Have I checked carefully for the proper use of capital letters?
- Have I checked carefully for words left out?
- Have I used a good range of vocabulary (rather than repeating the same words)?
- Have I avoided my previous mistakes?
- Do all my sentences actually make sense?
- Is each major idea developed in a separate paragraph?

a29: PROOFREADING

The passage below contains several mistakes. Read it carefully, circle each error and see how many you can find. Then say how each one should be corrected.

For his project Joe worked in a gruop to make and sell items to raise money for a Charity. Joe designed and made mugs with an image represnting the Charity. Other people in teh group made badge's, keyrings cards and jewlry.

Joe drew several different designs and asked people in his school and at home which one they liked best. he decided to use the design that most people prefered.

Next Joe tried out diffrent ways to put the design on the mug Then he carried out did some tests to see which gave the best-looking results and which were damaged least when the mugs were washed. Then he found out about cost of making the mug and decided how much to charge for them. Then he made twenty mugs with with the best design and sold them. Joes mugs raised £19.20 for the Charity.

PROJECT SPRINGBOARD

Fundraising for a charity or club, or for your school, could provide a starting point for a Project.

a30: WELL WRITTEN?

As you write up your Project, keep the LOISPaCER checklist in mind. When you have written the Research section, put it aside for a day then proofread it with fresh eyes to check that it still makes sense.

If possible, exchange drafts with someone else in your class. Give each other some feedback on the writing – be polite but honest! Then act on the feedback.

4.5 All my own work

Plagiarism

To get your Project qualification, you and your teacher/tutor have to sign a statement saying that your Project is all your own work. When you write up your Project, you can use books and the Internet but you must be careful to avoid **plagiarism**, which means copying someone else's work and pretending it is your own. If you do this, you will get no marks.

a31: WHAT'S WRONG WITH PLAGIARISM? TW EP E

In a small group, discuss why plagiarism is wrong. To help your discussion, think how you would feel if you found someone had passed off your work as their own. Think what might happen if someone such as a doctor (Figure 4.3) gained a qualification using someone else's work instead of their own.

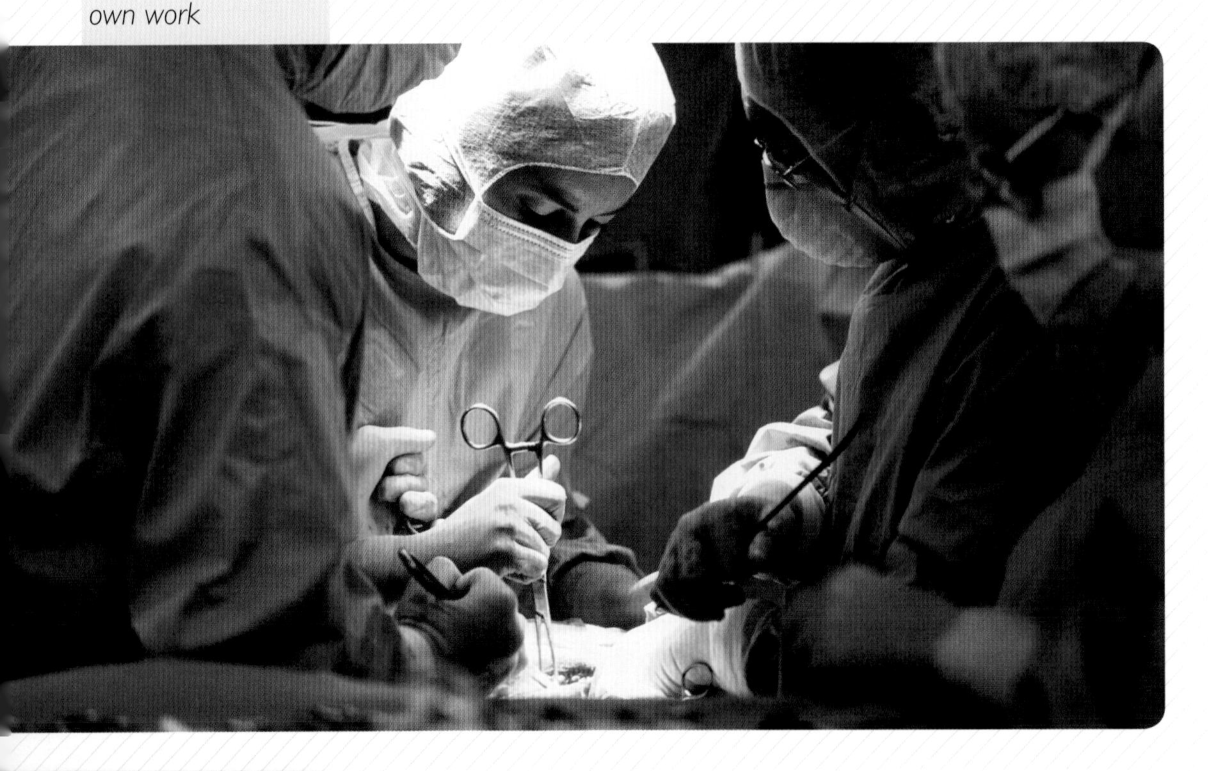

Figure 4.3
We need to be sure that people's qualifications are awarded for their own work

COURSE REF.

Use the thinking skills you developed in Lesson 2.3 to help your discussion.

There are two ways to avoid plagiarism:

- Write in your own words.

OR

- Make it clear you are quoting someone else's work and say where you got it from.

In your own words

In order to put things in your own words, you have to understand what you are writing about. Even then, it can be hard to use your own words when you have someone else's in front of you. To help, take the following steps when you are reading and gathering information.

Scan
Just look quickly at the page or paragraph, noticing headings, pictures and key words. Try to get an overall impression.

Question
Based on your overall impression, think how you might answer the '5 W' questions.

Read
Read the text carefully. Try not to slow up too much for difficult words; their meaning may become clear later on.

Remember
Without looking at the text, jot down the points that you can remember.

Review
Read the text again. Make some brief notes.

Write
Look away from the text. Write the information in your own words, just using your notes and what you can remember.

COURSE REF.

For more on the '5 W' questions see Lesson 1.1.

a32: IN YOUR OWN WORDS

Using the steps set out above, use your own words to write down the information from one of the sources you are using for your Project.

4.6 Name your sources

References

Sometimes in a written report you need to quote exactly what someone else has said or written. When you do this, make sure it is clear what you are doing. Put quote marks round the passage, or perhaps put it in a different font or a different colour. Then give a **reference** for your source, which means saying exactly where you got it from.

It is also important to give a reference even if you are not quoting. Unless you are using your own primary research, you need to say exactly where you got your information.

You can use your Research Record Sheets to record the details of each source you use. In a reference, you need to list the following information.

Books

Name of author(s), book title, name of publisher, year of publication, chapter number, page number(s).

You can find the details of the publisher and date on a page near the front or back of the book.

Magazines, journals and newspapers

Name of author(s), title of article, name of magazine, journal or newspaper, date, volume number (and issue number if given), page number(s).

Details of volume and issue number are usually given on the contents page and/or in the header or footer running along the top or bottom of each page.

Websites

Name of author, editor or organisation, date when the site was last updated, title of site, web address, date when you used the site.

Ideally you should give all these details, but many websites do not include such full information. List as much as you can find.

Bibliography

A bibliography is a list of all references you have used. It comes at the end of a report and follows the styles given above for the different sources.

A **footnote** lets you put the reference at the foot of the page[1] where it can be clearly seen but does not interrupt the flow of what you have written. If you are using Word on a PC, you can make a footnote by choosing Insert on the main toolbar, then Reference followed by Footnote. From the 'numbering' menu choose 'continuous' so that the program will automatically give each new footnote a new number. Click Insert and type in the information.

PROJECT HIN

Your references and bibliography will help you demonstrate good communication skills.

A **bibliography** (Figure 4.4) is neatest if it is in alphabetical order, or in the order that you use each reference.

Jenifer Burden, Anna Grayson, Angela Hall and Pam Large, Twenty First Century Science (GCSE Biology), 2006, Oxford University Press, Chapter B6 pages 164-173

Andy Coghlan, 'Brain cell injection boosts memory in mice', New Scientist, 10 November 2007, vol 196, issue 2629, p10

Stephen Robb, 'How a memory champ's brain works', BBC News magazine, updated 7 April 2009, http://news.bbc.co.uk/1/hi/magazine/7982327.stm, accessed 12 April 2009

Figure 4.4 *Part of a bibliography*

a33: FOOTNOTES AND BIBLIOGRAPHY

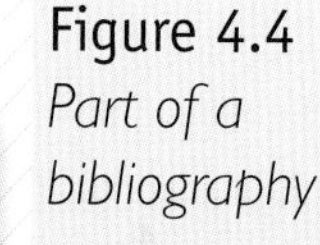

Go through your draft of the Research section of your report and put in footnotes to give references for all your sources. Then make a bibliography listing all the sources you have used so far.

4.7 Development

After the Research section comes the part of your Project where you develop your ideas and skills, and try out different approaches to your objective. For most projects this is the section that will take the most time. As you work on the Development, remember the golden rules:

- Keep your records up to date.
- Write up as you go along.
- Focus on your Project objective.

1 This is a footnote.

PROJECT HINT

The Development section is the main part where you show how you can develop and realise your Project work.

COURSE REF.

For more on thinking skills see Lesson 2.4.

Primary research

If you have carried out any primary research and collected your own data, this is where you write about what you have learned from the research. You should:

- state your final result(s)
- describe any trends or patterns
- point out anything you found that was unexpected
- suggest reasons and explanations for your results
- say how your own research relates to other work that you found out about in your secondary research
- say how your research relates to your Project objective.

Depending on what else you need to put in the Development section, you might need to put the discussion of your primary research under a separate heading.

COURSE REF.

For more on designing and making artefacts see Lesson 2.1.

Artefact

If you are producing an artefact, this is where you try out various ways of doing things, using different materials and techniques.

Your records will probably be mostly in the form of sketches, photographs and models (Figure 4.5). Make sure you keep them in a safe place, with dates and notes to remind you how your Project developed.

If you use a sketchbook, it should be either A4 or A3. Avoid layering images and keep any notebooks separate (don't attach them to the sketchbook). Single sheets or items should be no bigger than A1 in size.

Figure 4.5 *Models and sketches provide a record of your work*

If you are making a 3D object, you will need to take photographs to show work in progress and the final outcome.

When making a photographic record you should:

- use lighting to make sure that key features can be seen clearly
- show construction and materials
- show any important use of colour or texture
- take photographs from different angles
- clearly indicate the actual size of the object
- include information about scale if you are making a small-scale model
- use no more than five photographs to show the final outcome.

In your written report you should:

- describe your artefact (use photographs and sketches)
- say why you made it
- if necessary, explain how to use it or how it works
- say how your research has helped you design and make your artefact
- give an account of the decisions you made
- give reasons for your decisions
- give details of the materials you used
- give details of the techniques you used
- say how your artefact relates to your Project objective and design brief.

Your written report should mention any models you have used, and include photographs and sketches. This section might not need so many words because you are using sketches and other images.

Event

For a Project that leads to an event, this is where you explore various approaches and work out different techniques. If you are working on a group performance, make sure that each person's role is clear; you should each contribute about five minutes to the final performance.

COURSE REF.

For more on organising events see Lesson 2.2.

To record work in progress you might use video, DVD or CD along with photographs and notes. Make sure these are labelled and kept in a safe place.

In your written report:

- describe the event and your own role in it
- say where and when the event took place, and who took part
- say why you put on this event
- say how your research has helped with the event
- give reasons for your decisions
- give details of any technical resources you used
- say how the event relates to your Project objective.

Your written report should mention any DVDs and so on that provide a record of your work. This section might not need so many words because your work is recorded in other ways.

Written Project

If you are working on a written Project, this is where you explore your research question in depth. You need to develop you own point of view and set out reasons to support it.

COURSE REF.

For more on written Projects, see Lesson 2.3.

In your report you should:

- state your own point of view on your research question
- give reasons for your point of view
- state some other possible points of view
- give reasons for those points of view
- say how your research has helped you tackle your question.

a3 4: WORK IN PROGRESS 

When you have done some work on the development of your Project, discuss your progress with your teacher/tutor and with other people in your class. Listen to other people's comments and use them to help you keep your work on track.

4.8 What do you think?

Look back to your Project Proposal Form and remember why you chose your Project topic or research question. Before you started, you might have already had some firm ideas about the answer to your question (or how best to make an artefact or organise an event). Or perhaps you prefer just to say that one approach or answer is a bit better than another. However you express it, your Project will be much stronger if you can say clearly what you really think about your topic. You need to have a clear point of view.

COURSE REF.

For more on thinking skills see Lesson 2.4.

When taking part in an argument (Figure 4.6), some people can only see things from their own point of view. They cannot understand the opposite side at all. Other people shrug their shoulders and say that we can never know what to believe because there are always good arguments on both sides.

The best approach lies between these extremes. In the Development section of your project, you should consider both sides of any question, because people who think deeply about the issues can reach different conclusions. But it is important that you form you own point of view and try to justify it. It might seem as though you are being fairer by just stating both sides of the argument. In reality, though, you will learn more and understand the issues better if you try to argue for your own point of view.

a35: FIRST THOUGHTS

Reread your Project proposal, then briefly explain to others in your class what your topic is and what your own ideas are.

Figure 4.6
Taking part in an argument

Exploring your point of view

People hold all sorts of opinions on ethical and other questions but their ideas are often quite vague. Your Project gives you a chance to sort out your ideas and develop some thinking skills. In a written Project, exploring and developing your ideas is a big part of your work.

When you are thinking about your research question, it helps to go through the following stages.

Start by saying what your own ideas are

You have already done this on your Project Proposal Form and in Activity 34. Try to explain your ideas clearly.

Find out how other people have thought about your question

COURSE REF.

See Lesson 4.2 for more on the sorts of reasons people might give.

This is where your research is important. You need to do quite a bit of secondary research and read what other people have said and written about your question (or similar questions). You could also do some primary research and ask people for their views.

You will probably find that most people give one of just two or three main answers. Look for the reasons that they give. Do some people come to the same answer for different reasons? When you write up your Development section, you could deal with each main answer separately and set out various people's reasons for giving it.

One way to present these ideas is to use a **mind map** (Figure 4.7). Write your research question in the middle of a large sheet of paper, and write each main answer in a 'bubble' close to the edge. Then add notes to show how different reasons lead to each answer.

Think again about your own point of view

Do you still think the same as when you started? If so, can you give any more reasons to support your view?

Have you changed your mind? If so, what are your reasons for changing?

Figure 4.7
A mind map

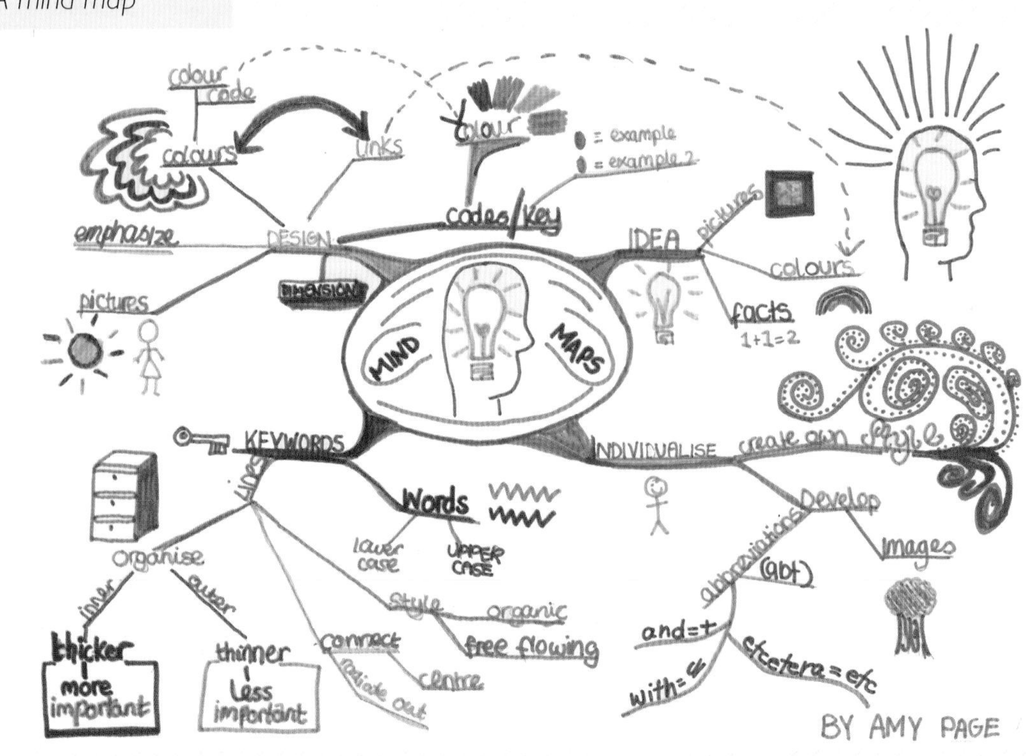

a36: MIND MAP

When you have done some research into your question, make a mind map to summarise the different ways people think about it.

a37: WHAT DO YOU THINK?

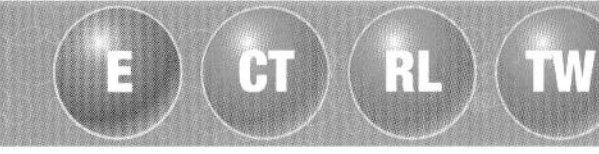

Using a copy of the questionnaire in Table 4.4, work with a partner to interview each other about your research questions.

When you are the interviewer, write down your partner's answers in the spaces provided.

After you have been interviewed, look at your own answers that your partner has written down. Use them as a guide to help you think how to put your ideas across as clearly as possible.

Discuss both sets of answers with your partner. Try to make helpful suggestions to each other – be positive rather than critical.

Your name: Your partner's name:
1. What is your partner's research question?
2. What is your partner's point of view about their research question?
3. What points of view do other people have?
4. What reasons does your partner give for their own point of view?
5. How could your partner explain their point of view more clearly?

Table 4.4
What do you think?

5 Final stages

5.1 Looking back, looking forward

Introduction revisited

When you have finished the Research and Development sections, you need to review your Project. First look at your Project Proposal Form and the draft of your Introduction (Lesson 4.1) and think about how your Project developed. At this stage you might need to rewrite the Introduction so that it describes what you actually did rather than what you thought you were going to do.

a38: INTRODUCTION REVISITED 

Go back to your draft Introduction and see if it describes what you actually did. Rewrite it if you need to.

Review

The Review section of your report should tell the 'story' of your Project. To write your Review section you need to look both backwards and forwards.

Look back over your Project and think about how you have changed your ideas, increased your knowledge and understanding and learned new skills. Also think about how your Project fits in with your other areas of study, your other subjects, or your plans for what you want to do next.

Your Review should include an **evaluation** where you think about the experience of doing Project work and reflect on how it went. You will have learned about doing research, organising your work and managing your time. Think about what worked well and what could have been done better.

Looking forwards, think about what else you might do for your Project if you had more time.

It is a good idea to talk through your Project with someone else (Figure 5.1) before you start to write the Review section. This can help you think clearly about the key points of your work.

What to include in your Review

The things you include in your Review section will depend partly on the type of Project you have done. Use this checklist as a guide.

Artefact

- Did you fulfil your design brief?
- Comment on the main features of your artefact.

Event

- Was your event successful?
- Comment on the main features of your event.

Written Project

- What is your answer to your research question?
- Summarise your main reasons for your answer.

All Project types

- Have you met your objective?
- What were the main things you learned from your research?
- What were the main skills you developed? In what ways have your ideas changed?
- How does your project work link to other areas of study and/or your future plans?
- What worked well and what didn't work so well in your Project?
- If you had more time, what else would you do?
- What did others think about your Project? Do you agree?

COURSE REF.

For guidance on length, see Lesson 4.1.

Figure 5.1
Talking about your Project

a39: REVIEW   E RL TW

With another member of your class, talk through your Project and try to answer the questions set out above.

Then write the Review section of your Project report.

5.2–5.3 Presentation

As part of your Review you might be asked to present your work to a group of other people. This could involve:

- a talk to an audience (Figure 5.2)
- a display where you talk to visitors.

Figure 5.2 *Talking to an audience*

Presenting your Project to other people can be scary but it does make you think carefully about your work and helps develop your communication skills.

Speaking out

If you are asked to talk about your work to a group of people, here are some tips:

- Plan what you are going to say.
- Use visual aids.
- Practise your talk.

Plan

Don't try to say too much. You will only have a few minutes to speak and you can't cover everything. Base your talk on the Review of your Project, and use the lists in Lesson 5.1 as a guide. Plan your talk in four parts.

Plan your talk in four parts

You should aim to:

- say what you set out to do (your Project objective)
- describe or state your project outcome (your artefact, event, or the answer to your research question)
- summarise the main things you learned
- say what went well, what could have been better and what else you would do if you had time.

For each part, make notes on your main points. Then for each point write a few words on a card in large clear letters. Number the cards in order. Hold the cards in your hand as you talk and glance down to remind yourself what to say next. As you finish each point, move the card to the back of the pack.

Visual aids

Make some visual aids for your talk. They will help you keep on track and will make sure your audience sees, as well as hears, your main points. They also give your audience something to look at other than you, which can be a great help if you are nervous.

For your visual aids, you could use PowerPoint or overhead slides. The golden rule is:

- Keep it simple.

Make one slide for each of the four parts of your talk, plus one more to show a picture of your Project outcome if it is an artefact or event, and one to show a graph or a chart of your main result if you did any primary research.

Keep the content clear and simple (Figure 5.3 (a) and (b)). People need to take it in at a glance, so use bullet points rather than long sentences. Use a large font (at least 24 pt).

Lyn Parkes

Project title
'Dancing round the world'

Group project
Research and perform different dance styles

My objectives
Find out about Japanese dance
Rehearse and perform a dance with my group

Figure 5.3 (a)
A good clear slide

How do you get to school?	Number of people
Bus	17
Train	13
Bike	9
Car	24
Walk	5

In my project I wanted to find out how to get more people coming to school by **bike** instead of coming by car.
I found that a lot of people think coming by bike is unsafe. So I think we could get the police to come and give some safety training and show people how they can cycle safely wearing reflective jackets and knowing the rules of the road.
I think we should have more bike sheds at school so people can keep their bikes and not worry they will be stolen.

What stops you coming by bike?	Number of people
Too far	14
Not safe	28
Don't have a bike	13
Too much to carry	12
Arrive hot and sweaty	8
Nowhere safe to keep bike at school	15

Figure 5.3 (b)
A cluttered, messy-looking slide

Visit the room where you will be talking and check that you know how to use any equipment such as a data projector.

Practice

When you have prepared your talk, practise it out loud. Either do this in a room on your own, or to a small group of people from your class. Try to do it 'for real', so don't keep stopping and starting, or asking people how it's going.

Even if you have prepared your talk well, you will probably be nervous. This is quite normal! Even experienced speakers such as actors, teachers, broadcasters and politicians can get nervous before speaking to an audience. The trick is to pretend you are calm, then that's how you will appear.

Do it for real

- Before you start, take a few deep breaths.
- Smile at your audience.
- Look around at your audience while you are speaking.
- Try to vary your pace and expression.
- Slow down if you hear yourself talking too fast. Don't be afraid to pause between the main points of your talk while you move to the next slide.
- End by thanking your audience.

PROJECT HINT

A well-planned talk will help you demonstrate good organisational and communication skills.

a40: TELLING A STORY

You will be given about five overhead transparencies in a random order. Decide how to arrange them to tell a story. Then use them to tell the story to other people.

a41: SPEAKING OUT

SM

Make a set of cards to summarise your talk about your Project, and a set of PowerPoint or overhead slides. Practise your talk.

On display

A display can be a good way to communicate your Project outcome, particularly if you have made an artefact. Here are some tips for a good display:

- Plan what you want your visitors to see.
- Use posters and labels to help make your points.

Plan

You will probably not have much space, so think about what's best to display. Think about how to show the 'story' of your Project.

Your display should include

- your final outcome (your artefact)
- items that show how your work developed (e.g. models, sketches).

You also need to include:

- your Project objective (your design brief)
- your evaluation of what went well, what could have been better and what else you would do if you had time.

Put these onto a poster or in a handout, and be prepared to talk about them to people visiting your display.

Visit the display venue in advance and find out how much space you will have.

Think about the layout of your display. You might want people to notice some things first (e.g. your final artefact) so plan the layout accordingly.

Posters and labels

The golden rule here is:

- Keep it simple.

People need to read posters and labels from a distance so use bullet points and single words rather than long sentences. Use a large font (at least 24 pt).

If you have items that show how your work developed, number them in order so that people can see the 'story' of your Project.

a42: ON DISPLAY CT SM

Choose the items that you will display. Decide how to use them to tell people about your Project. Make labels and posters. Plan the layout of your display.

PROJECT HINT

A well-planned display will help you demonstrate good organisational and communication skills.

5.4 Project record

You will need to hand in a record of your Project to be marked. Some records from your class will be sent off to a moderator to check that the marking is fair. Your Project record needs to contain evidence of your work and it must be well organised so that people can see exactly what you have done.

You need to hand in:

- your Project Proposal Form
- your Project planner (base this on the record in your project planner)
- your Project outcome
- your written report
- your artefact, or photographs of your artefact
- a recording of your performance on DVD, video or CD
- your evaluation (this can be part of your written report)
- your Candidate Record Sheet signed by you and your teacher/tutor to say your Project is all your own work.

Before you hand everything in, it is well worth checking carefully to make sure your report is complete and well written, and that all the other evidence for your outcome is in place.

Artefact records

For an artefact, in addition to your written report you need to hand in your finished artefact (or photographs of it) and evidence of your development work.

A well-organised Project record will help you demonstrate that you have managed your Project skilfully.

a43: ARTEFACT RECORDS SM

Use the checklist questions below to make sure you have everything that you need to hand in.

- For a 2D artefact, does it pack flat into a size no greater than A1?
- Is it packed so that it does not smudge or stick to anything?
- For a 3D artefact, do you have no more than five photographs showing its key features?

- For a computer-based artefact, have you recorded a working version on CD?
- Have you included evidence of your development work? e.g.
  - an A3 or A4 sketchbook
  - design development sheets no larger than A1
  - photographs of any models you used.
- Is everything labelled with your name and candidate number?

Event records

a44: EVENT RECORDS SM

Use the checklist below to make sure you have everything that you need to hand in.

If your Project outcome was an event, you need to provide evidence of the event and your development work.

- For a performance, do you have an unedited recording of the final event on DVD, video or CD?
- In the recording, do you introduce yourself clearly by name, state your candidate number and say what your role is?
- For a drama performance, does the recording include a full-length shot of your whole group?
- Have you included evidence of your development work? For example:
  - rehearsal schedules
  - letters and emails making arrangements.
- Is everything labelled with your name and candidate number?

Written report

If you have done a written Project, your written report will be your only outcome. If your Project led to an event or artefact, you still need to hand in a written report along with other evidence of your work; your written report will be shorter because you have provided other evidence of your work.

The Project examiners give some general advice about written reports. They should be on A4 paper, held together with tags (pieces of string that thread through punched holes). They should **not** be in file covers, binders or plastic pockets.

PROJECT HINT

A well-presented report will help you demonstrate good communication skills.

a4.5: CHECKING YOUR WRITTEN REPORT RL SM

Use the checklist questions below to make sure your report contains everything that it needs to, and that things are in the correct sections.

Introduction (See Lesson 4.1)

- Have you stated your Project objective, included your design brief or research question and given your reasons for choosing your Project?

Research (See Lessons 1.1, 1.2 and 4.3)

Secondary/background research

- Have you told the 'story' of what you found from your secondary research?
- Have you included key dates and people?
- Does the story relate clearly to your Project objective?
- Have you included references for all your sources?
- Have you commented on your sources? (You only need to do this at Level 2.)

Primary research (See Lessons 1.3–1.5 and 4.3)

- Have you described how you carried out any primary research?
- Have you included graphs and charts of your data?
- Have your described how you analysed your data?
- Have you stated your main results?

Development (See Lessons 4.7 and 4.8)

All project types

- Have you clearly described what you did, what decisions you made and given reasons for your decisions?
- Have you described how your ideas changed, how your skills developed and said what you learned from your research?

Artefact

- Have you said how you fulfilled your design brief, described different materials and techniques that you tried out and included photographs and sketches?

Event

- For a group Project, have you clearly described your own role and the different approaches that you tried out?

Written Project

- Have you answered your research question, given reasons for your answer and discussed other possible answers to your question?

Review (See Lesson 5.1)

- Have you given a clear summary of how you met your objective?
- Have you said how your skills and ideas have developed?
- Have you said what worked well and what could be better?
- Have you said what you would do if you had more time?

References and bibliography (See Lesson 4.6)

- Have you included references to all your sources, used footnotes or brackets to provide references and listed your sources in your bibliography?

General (See Lesson 4.1 and 4.4)

- Is your report a suitable length?
- Have you proofread your report?
- Have you provided a title page with your name, Project title and candidate number?
- Have you numbered your pages?
- Have you provided a list of contents?
- Have you tagged all your pages together?

And finally ...

Keep a copy of your Project in a safe place. Sometime in the future you might want to build on the work you have done, or show your Project to a possible employer, or talk about it in an interview for a course of study.

Glossary

Argument A set of statements and reasons explaining why a particular point of view is a good one, or why a particular conclusion is correct.

Artefact Something that is designed and made.

Biased One-sided. A biased source mostly contains information that supports one particular belief or one particular point of view. The information is likely to be correct but incomplete.

Bibliography A list of references to all the information sources used in a project. It is usually placed in a separate headed section at the end of the project report.

Brief (for a project) Instructions setting out what a project should achieve or produce.

Closed question A question that can only be answered by choosing one or more answers from a set provided.

Conclusion A summary of the main thing(s) you have found out from some research.

Data Factual information from measurements or surveys, generally in the form of numbers.

Design brief Instructions setting out particular features that an artefact should have, how it will be used, and how it should be made.

Ethics Reasoned views about why certain actions are right and others are wrong.

Evaluate (a project) To think about and communicate what went well, what could have been better, and what you have learnt about doing project work.

Fact A statement that is definitely true. For example, it is a fact that in November 2008 Barack Obama was elected president of the United States of America.

Footnote A note placed at the foot of a page so that someone can easily look at it while reading the main text. In a Project report, footnotes can be used to give details about sources of information that were used to write the main text.

Leading question A question that is worded so as to encourage people to give a particular answer. An example of a leading question is 'Would you choose to travel by bicycle, rather than going by car which causes more pollution?'.

Milestone (in a project) The finishing of a task that is part of a project. For example, one project milestone might be to finish collecting everyone's answers to a questionnaire.

Mind map A chart showing relationships between ideas.

Objection A reason for disagreeing with a particular point of view.

Objective Goal. What you set out to achieve.

Open question A question worded so that someone can think up their own answer and respond however they wish.

Outcome The end result of a project, or of a course of action. In a project, the outcome might be an artefact, an event or a written report. In ethics, considering the likely outcomes is one way to decide whether an action is right or wrong.

Plagiarism Using someone else's work or ideas and pretending they are your own. Copying something and not saying where it is from.

Point of view An opinion about a question or a course of action, supported by reasons.

Primary research Research that you carry out yourself, for example using experiments, measurements or questionnaires.

Proof-reading Checking a document to make sure that it is well organised and well written, with all the necessary material in a sensible order and with correct spelling, puncuation and grammar.

Questionnaire A set of questions designed to gather information and opinions from several people about a particular topic.

Reason A statement explaining why you hold a particular point of view, or why you acted in a particular way.

Reference Details of an information source. A reference must contain enough detail for someone else to find the source in a library or on the Internet.

Reliable Can be trusted to be correct.

Religious rules Rules set out in religious texts such as the Bible or the Qur'an. In ethics, religious rules are used by some people to decide whether a particular action is right or wrong.

Research A careful and organised search for information.

Rights Things that should nearly always be allowed. For example, most people believe that humans have the right to life, the right to a fair trial, and so on. In ethics, ideas about rights can help people decide whether a particular action is right or wrong.

Secondary research Finding out about work that other people have done, or the ideas they have had about a topic.

Significance Meaning. The extent to which a conclusion is likely to be correct and reliable.

Source (of information) Anything or anyone that provides information such as a book, website, magazine, experiment, questionnaire, expert person.

Timeline A chart showing dates when certain actions should be, or were, carried out, or dates when certain events took place.

Tables are indexed as, for example, 41t.